BEARING WITNESS

GENOCIDE AND ETHNIC CLEANSING IN THE MODERN WORLD™

THE NAZI REGIME AND THE HOLOCAUST

ZOE LOWERY and JAMES NORTON

ROSEN PUBLISHING

NEW YORK

Published in 2017 by The Rosen Publishing Group, Inc.
29 East 21st Street, New York, NY 10010

Library of Congress Cataloging-in-Publication Data

Names: Lowery, Zoe, author. | Norton, James R., author.
Title: The Nazi regime and the Holocaust / Zoe Lowery and James Norton.
Description: New York, NY : The Rosen Publishing Group, Inc., [2017] | 2017
  | Series: Bearing witness: genocide and ethnic cleansing in the modern
  world | Includes bibliographical references and index.
Identifiers: LCCN 2015049687 | ISBN 9781508171638 (library bound)
Subjects: LCSH: Germany—History—1933–1945—Juvenile literature. | National
  socialism—Juvenile literature. | Holocaust, Jewish (1939-1945)—Juvenile
  literature.
Classification: LCC DD256.5 .L686 2016 | DDC 940.53/18—dc23
LC record available at http://lccn.loc.gov/2015049687

Manufactured in China

CONTENTS

One death is a tragedy. A million deaths is just a statistic." This seems like a harsh statement—and it is. During the Second World War, Joseph Stalin, who was accountable for the deaths of millions of people living in the Soviet Union, made this blunt but astute statement. He recognized that as soon as the fatalities spiked to unfathomable statistics, people became numb to genocide, or the intentional killing of a certain group of people based on ethnicity, religion, race, or politics. As Merriam-Webster's online dictionary defines it the Holocaust was, "the mass slaughter of European civilians and especially Jews by the Nazis during World War II," and the mastermind behind it was Germany's Adolf Hitler. Discussions regarding the Holocaust often reference the figure six million because historians believe that somewhere between five and six million Jews were killed during the Holocaust, a number roughly the same as the population of Dallas-Fort Worth, according to WorldAtlas.com.

The sordid tale of the Holocaust (also called Shoah in Hebrew) is more than just figures. Its sheer scale makes it difficult to understand and grasp. But few things are as important as ensuring that the Holocaust's history is understood so we can commit it to memory and honor those who died and avoid such atrocities in the future.

A twistedly well-oiled mass killing machine, the Holocaust involved intricate routes for its vehicles, specifically coordinated military divisions, roll calls and population lists, and a complete force to supervise, patrol, put people to death, and dispose of the cadavers. They managed this in the thick of the Second World War, when Nazi Germany's soldiers were in high demand to fight the Soviet Union, Great Britain, and the United States. The Nazis' thirst for blood and pure loathing for Jews was so powerful, however, that it committed valuable people to construct, manage, and maintain the concentration camps where not only Jewish people, but other minorities including Catholics, Gypsies, homosexuals, and other so-called "inferior" groups, were held captive and slaughtered. Rather than focus their efforts against the United States, Britain, and the Soviet Union, Germany felt that the Jewish people were the far greater foe and a serious menace.

The Sculpture of Love and Anguish is located in Miami Beach, Florida, and is just one of many Holocaust memorials around the world.

Jews lived fairly normal lives before Adolf Hitler and his Nazi Party came to power. They were property owners, married whomever the liked—even non-Jewish Germans—were employed at top colleges, held political positions in government, and served in the German military. In short, most Jews considered themselves to have effectively become a part of German society. Many thought of themselves as Germans before they thought of themselves as Jews. Hitler's violent leadership would put an end to these inclusive feelings.

During the Holocaust (1930s–1945) the Nazis and their allies executed between five and six million Jewish people, mostly in Germany and eastern Europe. Nevertheless, today the debate still rages over how the Holocaust began and why no one stepped forward to put an end to it. Unquestionably, Adolf Hitler's ascent to power with his National Socialist (or Nazi) Party in Germany was the first action to trigger the chain of events that resulted in humankind's greatest and most methodical mass murder.

CHAPTER 1

HITLER'S ASCENT TO POWER

O n April 20, 1889, young Adolf Hitler came into the world in Austria. As the First World War broke out in 1914, Hitler was living there and fought in the German army. Hitler as well as many Germans felt that the downfall of Germany was thanks to the treachery of feeble political leaders and other opponents of the state. Unfortunately, the German Jews stood out among the population

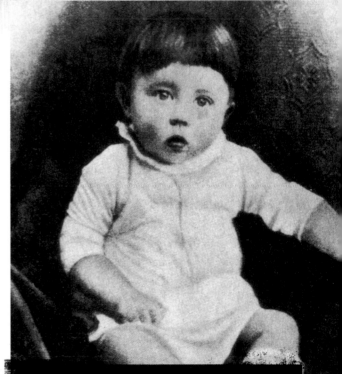

Adolf Hitler (pictured here about 1890) was born in Austria on April 20, 1889. As a young student, he often dreamed of becoming a painter.

and became common objects for blame. Hitler (and others) blamed them for destabilizing the war effort as well as shying away from the front lines by working in sheltered positions.

There is no historical evidence for this accusation whatsoever. Jews served with bravery in the German military, undertaking dangerous frontline jobs in large numbers and often receiving medals for their efforts. Many died or were wounded in action. But because they had a different ethnic and religious identity from that of most Germans, they became a convenient scapegoat for blame. In later years, during the Nazi regime, even Jews who had been decorated German officers would find that their patriotism was no shield. The only thing that mattered to the Nazis was that a person was Jewish, and that identification often served as a death certificate.

THE NAZI PARTY ON THE RISE

After World War I came to an end in November of 1918, Adolf Hitler became involved in German politics, joining a small right-wing party called the German Workers' Party. Its members were angry about the treaty that ended World War I, called the Treaty of Versailles. The treaty required Germany to pay money to the victorious Allied powers (including France and Britain), took various territories from Germany, and imposed limits on the German armed forces. All of this was seen as an outrage to German honor. A group of Germans called the November Criminals was blamed for stabbing the army in the back. A combination of Communists, Jews, and weak politicians were all blamed for the surrender, which was in fact a result of the inferiority of Germany's military and economy to those of the Allied powers that opposed them.

By July of 1921, Hitler had seized control of the German Workers' Party, now called the National Socialist, or Nazi, Party. Hitler was an impressive speaker. Emotional, sarcastic, passionate, and filled with rage, he could hold a room full of people at attention for hours at a time. Although he was seen as an unimportant figure by the country's major right-wing politicians, they often harnessed his passion and dedicated followers to suit their purposes. The Nazis could stir up street violence and push for radical right-wing solutions that more mainstream politicians could not or would not advocate, and they represented a small but increasingly vocal and influential number of voters on election day.

At first, Hitler and the Nazis were not interested in winning power peacefully or through a legitimate electoral process; there were too many obstacles to clear and too many more powerful and popular parties to beat. The seizure of Italy's government in 1922 by Fascist leader Benito Mussolini inspired Hitler and his followers to attempt a similar grab at power in Germany. On November 8, 1923, the Nazi Party attempted to take over the major German state of Bavaria, but the attempt was a disaster. Sixteen Nazis were killed, the revolt was crushed by the military, and Hitler and other leading party leaders were put on trial.

HITLER'S STRUGGLE

Hitler turned his trial into a platform for his poisonous political philosophy. A sympathetic judge let him speak for hours about his plans for Germany. Although he was sentenced to five years in a comfortable prison, the trial turned him into a popular national celebrity. He was seen as a man of action and one of the only people brave enough to fight for Germany's honor and against the unpopular Treaty of Versailles. In prison, he visited with fellow jailed Nazis, read mail from like-minded admirers, and entertained guests. Meanwhile, he put his ideas into print, working on his autobiography. Entitled *Mein Kampf* ("My Struggle"), it told the story of Hitler's "heroic" fight against the enemies of Germany. In it, many future actions—including the persecution of Jews and his attempted conquest of Europe— were clearly discussed.

One of *Mein Kampf*'s central themes was how the weak or otherwise "unfit" should be sacrificed to benefit the good of the majority. Hitler wrote: "It is a half-measure to let incurably sick people steadily contaminate the remaining healthy ones. This is in keeping with the humanitarianism which, to avoid hurting one individual, lets a hundred others perish. The demand that defective people be prevented from propagating equally defective offspring is a demand of the clearest reason and, if systematically executed, represents the most humane act of mankind."

This sort of argument was the bedrock of Nazi theory, and *Mein Kampf* was full of it: essentially, that the weak should be sterilized or even eliminated (although Hitler was careful to avoid

Hitler posed for a series of photographs for Heinrich Hoffmann while listening to recordings of his own speeches. He later demanded that Hoffmann destroy the negatives, but Hoffmann did not.

explicitly calling for murder) in order that others may live and prosper. His willingness to label human beings as "defective" or un-German set the stage for the killings to come later on. And those who read between the lines of the book could find plenty of evidence that Hitler would take action to jail and even kill anyone who was seen as an enemy of Germany, including racial "enemies" such as the Jews.

Published in 1925 and 1926, *Mein Kampf* sold about 240,000 copies between 1925 and 1934. Eventually, after the Nazi takeover of the country, about ten million copies would be sold or handed out for free. *Mein Kampf* and Hitler's triumphant trial turned him into the undisputed leader of the Nazis. As a party, the Nazis moved from the freedom of having internal debates and elected leadership to a totalitarian system wherein Hitler's word was always final. Later, when the Nazis would eventually gain power in Germany, a similar shift—from democracy to dictatorship—would take place.

FUELING THE FLAMES OF HATRED

The Great Depression—a period of worldwide economic collapse that resulted in the impoverishment and ruin of millions of families—provided Hitler and the Nazis with a golden opportunity to seize power. Many Germans were unemployed. They were angry, desperate, and hungry. They wanted enemies to blame for their country's weakness and the collapse of the economy, and Hitler offered them someone to blame and hate. Aggressive campaigning built up the Nazi

GUIDING THE GESTAPO

As head of security under Hitler's government, Reinhard Heydrich (1904–1942) led the Reich Main Security Office, which included the notorious secret police known as the Gestapo. He was responsible for building the Gestapo into a terrifying weapon of state power. So cruel were his methods that even his fellow Nazis viewed him as a butcher.

Heydrich's most notorious contribution to the Holocaust was the chairing of the 1942 Wannsee Conference. At this gathering, plans were finalized for the destruction of all of Europe's Jews. Heydrich was shot by British-trained Czechoslovak soldiers in Prague on May 27, 1942, in an assassination attempt. He died a week later.

Reinhard Heydrich (pictured in 1942) was the cruel leader of the Reich Main Security Office in charge of the Sicherheitsdienst and the Gestapo.

Party's popularity even as the democratically elected government, known as the Weimar Republic, floundered in search of solutions. Hitler was a master of propaganda—the use of words, music, images, and other forms of communication to hammer home political messages. By playing on prejudice, fear, national pride, and hatred, he built up the Nazi Party into a national organization.

Hitler and the Nazis now ran energetically for political office, seeking to take power by legal means. Although the Nazis often fought in the streets with their political opponents (mostly with the Communists), they also fought at the ballot box. In 1932, Hitler campaigned by airplane—a first in Germany—and came in second in a national election. A once-marginal politician who stirred his audiences with a patriotism based upon prejudice and hatred had come to the forefront of the country with votes, not guns.

After another year of political wrangling, Hitler finally managed to get himself appointed chancellor of Germany on January 30, 1933. A month later, the Reichstag building—the "Congress" of Germany where elected representatives met to debate and vote on legislation—was set on fire, an act blamed on a Communist. This gave Hitler's new government the chance it was looking for to crack down on political opponents. The German Communist Party, the main rival to the Nazis, was banned. New elections

The 1933 fire in the Reichstag building gave Hitler's new government an opportunity to blame it on a Communist and go after political opponents, for instance by banning the German Communist Party.

undertaken in an atmosphere of fear gave the Nazi Party an even stronger hold on the government. Nazi laws eliminated or restricted civil liberties (such as a right to a fair trial and protection against being jailed without just cause).

Because Germans were scared of Communist terrorism (like the Reichstag fire, which was blamed on Communists) and wanted a strong leader to ensure the rebuilding of the armed forces greatly weakened by the Versailles Treaty, there was little resistance to the Nazi takeover. By August of 1933, with the death of the country's president (whose powers were then given to Hitler) and the passage of legislation making Hitler's power unquestionable, the Nazis had taken absolute control of Germany. The voters and other political parties (including the main Catholic party) had willingly given power to the Nazi Party in a time of trouble, and the Nazi Party had made that gift permanent. There would be no more challenge from opponents seeking to use elections to challenge Nazi ideas.

CHAPTER 2

PROMOTED PROPAGANDA

Jewish people started fleeing Germany almost as soon as the Nazi Party ascended to power. Around 37,000 German Jews escaped to other parts of the world, many of whom had connections around the world and/or wealth. The harsh anti-Semitic Nazi propaganda had persuaded numerous non-Jews that Jews were nothing more than leeches who took advantage of the work of others without giving anything back. They weren't even "real" Germans. According to Nazi propaganda, "real" Germans were tough, imaginative, faithful, healthy, and attractive, whereas Jews symbolized infection, gluttony, wickedness, and a fading of the national character.

This propaganda ignored the fact that Jews were in fact great contributors to German economic, intellectual, creative, and artistic vitality. Jews were professors, bankers, professional musicians, artists, craftspeople, factory workers, merchants, and scientists. Some of the most economically and culturally important people in the country were Jewish. This changed with the rise of the Nazis, however. Jews were encouraged—

POISONING THE ATMOSPHERE

Adolf Hitler's right-hand man and minister for propaganda, Dr. Paul Joseph Goebbels (1897–1945), is among those most responsible for the poisonous atmosphere that led to the marginalization, demonization, imprisonment, and death of six million of Europe's Jews. As editor of the Berlin Nazi newspaper *Der Angriff* ("The Attack") in the 1920s, Goebbels fought tirelessly to advance the Nazi cause, savagely attacking Jews and left-wing opponents while doing so. After the Nazis came to power in 1933, Goebbels organized a mass burning of books by Jewish and other "subversive" authors. He also drove Jews out of their jobs in journalism, film, publishing, music, and literature.

The first major event in Goebbels's long record of anti-Semitism was his organizing of the Kristallnacht

Paul Joseph Goebbels was responsible for presenting the Nazi Party in a positive light to the German public, in part as editor of a Nazi newspaper.

attacks of 1938. His attitude only hardened as the years went by. Writing in his diary in 1942, Goebbels was pitiless toward the Jews: "In general, it can probably be established that 60 percent of them must be liquidated, while only 40 percent can be put to work...A judgment is being carried out on the Jews which is barbaric, but fully deserved." At the war's end, as Allied forces seized Berlin, Goebbels and his wife, Magda, killed their six children before killing themselves.

sometimes with threats and violence—to leave the country. Jewish businesses were bought out by non-Jewish Germans, often because of threats and menacing by the police.

JEWISH GERMAN BOYCOTT

On April 1, 1933, Hitler declared a national boycott of Jewish businesses. The Nazi leadership suggested that Jews were "the guilty ones" responsible for the country's economic problems, who "live in our midst and day after day misuse the right to hospitality, which the German Volk [people] has granted them." The effects of the boycott were felt across the country. Jews who had lived for generations in Germany were made to feel as though they were no longer really Germans but were instead now considered foreigners who had worn out their welcome.

In *Holocaust: A History,* by Deborah Dwork and Robert Jan van Pelt, the authors tell the story of a Jewish family living in a

Members of the Schutzstaffel and Sturmabteilung posted signs urging Germans to boycott Jewish-owned businesses, blaming them for the economic problems of the country.

small southern German town: "In the morning before classes, we would all congregate in the Turnplatz [gym field] where we played. I remember the boys were on one side and the girls on the other side, and we were playing ball. We were standing there, these four girls, four of us, and no one ever threw the ball to us. That's when we knew. That was it. That day of the boycott, April 1, 1933, that was really the watershed. After that, it was as if we weren't there." Within weeks of the boycott, Jewish people were banned by law from working in the civil service (low-ranking government positions) and the legal profession. This was part of an emerging pattern: by removing Jews from positions of influence, from which they could speak out, it made Jews far less visible and far less able to object to the treatment they were receiving. Soon Jewish students were banned from public schools, and Jewish doctors were thrown out of national hospitals. The first step to destroying a people is to make them invisible, and this is a task that the Nazis undertook nearly as soon as they were elected.

At the same time that the Jews were being removed from public life and stripped of their rights, other segments of the German population were suffering under Nazi control. Forced sterilizations of the mentally handicapped, blind, deaf, mentally ill, and habitual criminals resulted in some 400,000 people being stripped of their ability to have children. All of this was part of the Nazi plan for a "master race." Germany, said Hitler, was to be the land of the "pure" and "superior" Aryans—northern Europeans such as Germans and Scandinavians. Slavic people (such as Russians and many eastern Europeans), Gypsies (Roma), Jews, those of African descent, and the mentally or physically handicapped were deemed to be "impure" and "inferior," and millions of them would be exterminated as a result.

SCARE TACTICS

Why did Germans go along with this deranged and nonsensical Nazi plan to create a false sense of racial purity? Hitler and his government aggressively worked to rebuild the country's armed

Much of the Nazi anti-Semitic propaganda was presented as though it were based on well-researched, factual information.

forces and reassert its power on the world stage. At a time of great confusion and ambivalence, Nazis offered strong, absolute, black-and-white answers. And anti-Semitism had been a force in Germany (and throughout all of Europe) for centuries. Although the Nazi brand of anti-Semitism was allegedly "scientific" and based on crackpot theories presented as though they were carefully researched, it tapped into old tribal fears about the neighbor who doesn't go to church and doesn't share all the same traditions as the German Catholic or Protestant family next door.

Many ordinary Germans were scared by the Nazis, who were happy to imprison those who spoke out. And many Germans saw an advantage to stripping the Jews of their power and property. Non-Jews stood to take their jobs, their homes, and their businesses. A combination of fear and greed undermined any help and protection these Germans might have offered to their Jewish neighbors. The Jews were left exposed and defenseless to Nazi harassment and violence.

WORSENING REPRESSION

In the years following the Nazi regime's rise to power, the persecution of Jews got worse. The government used something called the salami technique—discrimination enacted one thin slice at a time. By mid-1935, signs on shop windows declaring "Jews and dogs not welcome" and "No Jews served" became commonplace. Within a couple of years, what was once a thriving mainstream part of the German population had been removed from public life. Jews were thrown out of hospitals, courtrooms, universities, the armed forces, and almost any place that could be used as a platform for self-defense or pride.

Paradoxically, new Jewish cultural and religious associations sprung up in this hostile environment, and the identity of the community was actually strengthened by persecution. But

LIFE-SAVING LIST

Not all Germans aided the Nazis' Holocaust efforts or stood by silently and did nothing while the killing continued. Some worked against it. Oskar Schindler (1908–1974), an ammunition and enamelware manufacturer in Germany, is credited with saving 1,200 Jews by having them work in his factories. Schindler used his Nazi Party membership, charm, persuasion, bribes, and trickery to protect his Jewish workers and their families and to keep himself out of jail.

In 1993, Schindler's story reached much of the world by way of Steven Spielberg's Holocaust movie *Schindler's List*. Schindler's motives were unclear. But through the course of the war and the Holocaust, he was transformed from a self-interested businessman into the savior of more than a thousand lives. An interview with Schindler may reveal some of what motivated him to act: "I knew the people who worked for me...When you know people, you have to behave toward them like human beings" (as quoted in an article by the *Independent*).

these new associations couldn't protect Jews from the ferocity of an angry German government and people. More and more violent actions were taken against Jews. Germans wrecked Jewish shops, beat Jewish people, and took the law into their own hands. Police rarely, if ever, intervened to protect Jews from their former countrymen.

In 1936, Berlin hosted the summer Olympic Games, which led to a temporary die-down in anti-Jewish hostility as the world's eyes were turned to Germany. But things worsened again in 1937. The Nuremberg Rally, a massive party meeting in the German town of the same name, confirmed Hitler's plans to racially "unite" the country by removing the Jewish population. Under the slogan "Ein Reich, Ein Volk, Ein Fuhrer" ("One Empire, One People, One Leader"), Hitler asserted German racial power and vowed to bring all Germanic peoples together into one supercountry. This was followed in 1938 by the unification of Austria and Germany.

The German empire was growing. And as it did, more and more Jews became victims of its racism. In Austria, soon after German troops marched in, Jews were forced to clean the pavement on their hands and knees, using toothbrushes and a cleaning solution made with acid. Many were sent to concentration camps, which were at this point mostly holding pens for political prisoners and "undesirables." Although conditions were bad, the camps had not yet become places of mass death.

NIGHT OF BROKEN GLASS

A key turning point came on November 7, 1938. A young Jewish man named Herschel Grynszpan, angered over the expulsion of his parents from Germany, shot a German diplomat named Ernst vom Rath, who was stationed in Paris, France. The shooting was immediately reported by Nazi newspapers and turned into an excuse for a string of attacks on nearly ten

A YOUNG GIRL'S DIARY

Annelies Marie "Anne" Frank (1929–1945) was born in Frankfurt, Germany, in 1929. Born into a Reform Jewish family, her father was a decorated German officer from World War I—a fact that would do nothing to help the family during the Holocaust. Anne fled Germany with her family in early 1934 after the Nazi Party won local elections.

The Franks ended up in the Netherlands, a temporary safe haven for Jews. But the Nazis invaded and occupied the Netherlands in 1940. By July 1942, the family was living in a hiding place above her father's workplace. An informant's tip led to the family's arrest in 1944, and Anne and her sister were shipped off to Bergen-Belsen concentration camp. Both would die there in 1945. Her father, however, survived the ordeal and returned to Amsterdam. Having been informed of his daughters' deaths and recovering Anne's diary of their time in hiding, he fulfilled Anne's wish to become an author. In 1947, Anne Frank's diary was published.

Anne's observations about the ongoing Holocaust—the constant fear of discovery and arrest, the struggle to eat, the cruelty of ordinary people—were often dark. But she kept a sense of optimism even amid the darkest of circumstances: "I don't think of all the misery, but of the beauty that still remains...My advice is: 'Go outside, to the fields, enjoy nature and the sunshine, go out and try to recapture happiness in yourself and in God. Think of all the beauty that's still left in and around you and be happy!'"

thousand Jewish businesses and more than a thousand places of worship. The violence, which stretched across Germany, became known as Kristallnacht, the "Night of Broken Glass." Shop windows were shattered, homes were trashed by Germans wielding axes and clubs, Jews were imprisoned and beaten to death, Jewish cemeteries were vandalized, and more than 1,500 synagogues (Jewish temples) were burned.

Many historians say that Kristallnacht was the true beginning of the Holocaust, the moment in which the German

The ruins of Tielshafer Synagogue in Berlin are a haunting reminder of Kristallnacht, which many historians mark as the beginning of the Holocaust.

government's campaign against Jews moved from stripping them of their legal rights and driving them out of the country toward the destruction of property and extermination of people. The pretense that the German government was taking rights away from Jews in order to protect or shelter them had now fallen completely apart, and naked hatred had become the order of the day. Nazi police and special troops known as the SS (the "protective squadron" that was personally answerable to Hitler) helped organize Kristallnacht, and SS members would be the key leaders of later efforts to contain and then destroy Jews throughout Nazi-occupied Europe.

Increasingly after Kristallnacht, Jews were removed from their homes, stripped of their belongings, and shipped off to ghettos. Ghettos were special concentrations of city blocks walled off and restricted to Jews only. In cities such as Warsaw, Jews slept nine people to a room, a recipe for disease and misery. The concentration of Jews into ghettos helped non-Jews forget about their existence and made later steps—such as shipping them off in freight cars to concentration camps—much easier to accomplish.

CHAPTER 3

EXTERMINATION CAMPS

The places where millions of Jews were imprisoned and then killed are generally known as concentration camps. Camps built and used solely for killing prisoners were known more specifically as extermination or death camps. Built in the early days of the Nazi government, concentration camps were originally designed to hold political prisoners and other "undesirables" such as Roma, or Gypsies. Jews were sometimes rounded up and placed in these camps.

While conditions were often terrible, they weren't originally meant to hold prisoners for long periods of time, nor were they designed to be places where prisoners would be systematically killed. With the advent of the war, however, conditions in the camps began to change radically. Camps took on a role in the German economy, providing slave labor designed to help the war effort. Major German corporations willingly used this slave labor. It was cheaper than paying regular workers (who were in short supply following the outbreak of World War II) and was seen as patriotic.

Additionally, the camps began to fill with prisoners of war (mostly Soviet) who were treated extremely poorly. An estimated three million Soviet prisoners would die in camps before the end of war. Some estimates, accounting for prisoners shot on the spot by German troops, suggest that as many as five million Soviet prisoners were killed by the Nazis throughout the course of the war. As the fight against the Allies grew harder, the quest for the "Final Solution" became more desperate.

EXTERMINATION ONCE AND FOR ALL

The true turning point came in 1942, in a Berlin meeting known as the Wannsee Conference. This meeting, attended by high-level Nazi members of government, finally settled an argument that had been taking place among Hitler's advisers. Some of Hitler's ministers thought that Jews were best used as slave labor and a bargaining chip in case of an Allied victory. But a more influential group thought that the time had come to exterminate the Jews once and for all. The German governor of occupied Poland, Hans Frank, speaking a month before the conference, said, "We must destroy the Jews wherever we find them and wherever it is possible to do so" (according to public Nuremburg trial documents).

Tragically, Frank's remarks echoed the tone of the Wannsee meeting, which took place on January 20, 1942. Minutes of the meeting show a general agreement that the eleven to twelve million Jews throughout Europe (including portions not yet and never to be conquered by Germany) should be deported to

Occupied Poland's German governor Hans Frank is famous for uttering this chilling statement: "We must destroy the Jews wherever we find them and wherever it is possible to do so."

SECOND IN COMMAND

Heinrich Himmler (1900–1945) controlled the SS—Nazi Germany's elite armed police—and, to some degree, all of Germany's police and security forces during the war. He became the second most powerful person, after Hitler. Himmler was the founder and commander of the concentration camps and the Einsatzgruppen mobile death squads. He professed a belief in the superiority of the Aryan race and believed that selective breeding could engineer the German populace to be entirely "Nordic" in appearance within several decades.

On October 4, 1943, Himmler spoke explicitly about the ongoing killing of the Jewish people during an SS meeting in Poznan, Poland: "I also want to mention a very difficult subject before you here, completely openly. It should be discussed amongst us, and yet, nevertheless, we will never speak about it in public. I am talking about the Jewish evacuation: the extermination of the Jewish people" (according to a transcription of tape retrieved from the Nuremberg Trials). In 1945, he committed suicide after being captured by the British army.

camps to work in labor gangs, with the hope of working some if not most of them to death. The approval of a mass movement of Jews and the general agreement that death was an acceptable and even desirable end for them set the stage for the killing that was to come. Once it was agreed at the highest levels of Hitler's government that Jewish communities should be uprooted and put under the direct control of the SS, the crowding, disease, and eventual extermination of Jewish prisoners that followed was all but inevitable.

METHODICAL MURDERS

Before the Wannsee Conference had even happened, the Germans had been using poison gas vans and roving firing squads to kill Jews in occupied Russia and Poland. Nazi leaders such as Heinrich Himmler, Adolf Eichmann, and Reinhard Heydrich had approved of a campaign to kill Jews by whatever means necessary. This sometimes meant rounding up families of Jews, throwing them into locked air-tight vans, and then turning on a flow of poisoned gas. Sometimes the gas failed, leaving the people inside to die a slow death of suffocation.

Eventually, the gas vans fell out of use. Mobile firing squads called Einsatzgruppen killed an estimated 1.3 million Jews (according to historian Raul Hilberg) in countries such as Lithuania, Russia, Ukraine, and Poland. SS men and volunteers would shoot prisoners in groups and dump the bodies into long trench-like mass graves. Entire Jewish communities would be massacred like this, with women and children dying alongside men.

Deborah Dwork and Robert Jan van Pelt's book *Holocaust* lays out a bird's-eye view of Treblinka, one of the most deadly of the extermination camps, in early 1943. About three-quarters of a

Jews from the Ukraine and other countries were executed and their bodies pitched mercilessly into mass graves, which were mere pits in the ground.

million people were eventually killed at Treblinka, which was in peak operation from July 1942 through October 1943. Located northeast of Warsaw, Poland, it was centrally positioned to be a destination for Europe's Jews. The camp was surrounded by antitank defenses. Like all Nazi concentration camps, it was militarized so as to prevent escape from within or rescue from outside. A railway spur connected the camp to the main line of the railroad so that Jews and others could be brought into the camp in large numbers.

After arriving at the camp, valuables were taken from prisoners. Any who seemed as though they might resist were brought into a sham "hospital" and shot. Most of the new arrivals were brought to an undressing barracks, after which they were directed straight to the gas chambers. Carbon monoxide was then used to kill large groups of people at once. By the end of the camp's existence, it featured thirteen gas chambers. After victims were killed with gas, their gold teeth were extracted, and their bodies were burned on "roasts." The ashes were buried in mass graves. The cremation and burial portions of the camp were screened from the rest of the operation by earthen walls so as not to panic the prisoners. In addition to Treblinka, a number of other camps, including Chelmno, Belzec, and Sobibor, were solely used for killing. Auschwitz (with its satellite death camp of Birkenau) and Majdanek were built for other reasons, but they were eventually also transformed into execution sites.

The trauma suffered by families arriving at these camps cannot be overstated. Many knew or strongly suspected that death awaited them. Upon arriving at camps, most families were separated by guards. Helen Lebowitz Goldkind, a survivor of the Auschwitz camp who told her story on the U.S. Holocaust Memorial Museum's website, describes what it was like to arrive at the camp:

> *Then you see these mothers coming down with little kids, and they're...and they're trying to pull these kids out of their mother's hands…. It...it, there was so much screams. So, there was a truck….So, the parents, the...the mothers that wouldn't give up these children, and they, they were beaten up, and the kids got hurt, so they grabbed these*

Jewish mothers were ruthlessly separated from their children when they arrived at the Auschwitz concentration camp in Poland. Many were sent to die in the gas chambers.

kids, and they threw them on the truck, and they really didn't look how they were throwing them on the truck. ... And, of course, on that truck there were people, you know, very sick people going, you know, they were throwing sick people there, and...and...and these children that gave them a tough time.... And there were so many mothers that were running after the trucks, and, of course, they beat them, and they pushed them back.

While the gassing and cremation of prisoners was the most direct way that extermination camps were used to kill prisoners, many were killed in the camps by overcrowding, starvation, overwork, and disease. The very act of uprooting people from their homes and forcing them into inhumane conditions in camp was life-threatening, and many of the first victims were children and the elderly.

FIGHTING BACK

Although overwhelmed by the strength of the armed guards who patrolled the camps, Jews made many efforts to resist, staging uprisings in the death camps whenever possible. On August 2, 1943, prisoners at Treblinka seized weapons from the camp armory. Hundreds of prisoners stormed the main gate in an attempt to escape. Three hundred got out, but two-thirds of those who did were tracked down and killed by German SS and police units, as well as units from the German military.

A JEWISH RESISTOR

A Polish Jew born to a poor family near Warsaw, Morde-chaj Anielewicz (1919–1943) would grow up to become a

Some Jews fought back against the Nazis' cruel treatment. The Warsaw Ghetto Uprising was one attempt by the Jews to prevent more Jews from being sent to death camps.

leader in the fight against the Nazi occupation of Poland. As a young twenty-something, he became chief commander of the Jewish Fighting Organization in the Warsaw ghetto.

In January 1943, Anielewicz was instrumental in leading the fighting that would prevent a shipment of Jews from being deported from the ghetto into the concentration camps, where the Jewish prisoners would have been killed. This first ghetto uprising was followed by another fight that was finally put down by German forces in May of the same year. Anielewicz and his girlfriend, Mira Fuchrer, were both killed in the street battle, along with many of their comrades. He has been remembered as one of the heroes of the Holocaust for fighting a doomed fight—against extremely long odds—to keep Jews from being slaughtered by the Germans.

At Birkenau (the death camp of Auschwitz) on October 7, 1944, Jewish Sonderkommandos staged a revolt (Sonderkommandos were inmates put to work in the gas chambers and crematoria). They used axes, tools, rocks, and homemade grenades to take SS guards by surprise and destroy one of the crematoria. Although hundreds of prisoners escaped, all were soon recaptured. Many other armed resistance and escape attempts were made, although the vast majority failed. Starving, unarmed prisoners were usually no match for well-fed guards armed with machine guns.

A TRAITOR

The occupied peoples of Europe took a number of different stances toward the Nazi occupiers. Some governments fled and fought the Nazis from exile. Some government officials resigned, to be replaced by Germans. And some ordinary citizens from occupied countries collaborated, helping the Germans deport Jews and fight the war against the Allies.

Vidkun Quisling (1887–1945) was a Norwegian Fascist politician who welcomed the 1940 Nazi invasion of his country and became Norway's minister president under German rule. During his term of service, he was responsible for recruiting his fellow citizens to serve in the Norwegian SS division, deporting Jews (to almost certain death in concentration camps), and executing Norwegian patriots. After the war, Quisling was executed for treason. To this day, calling someone a Quisling is the same thing as calling the person a traitor.

It should be noted that in the rush to destroy Europe's Jews, many other groups of people were sacrificed to the Nazi death machine. Jehovah's Witnesses, Roman Catholic Poles, homosexuals, Roma, and many others were killed. And while many Jewish victims came from Germany and occupied Poland, many other Jewish prisoners came from Nazi-occupied countries like France, Hungary, Norway, and the Netherlands.

FREEDOM

For many imprisoned in the concentration camps, there was disbelief that the Allies hadn't done more to stop their suffering. U.S. planes could have bombed the trains leading to the camps. Although some prisoners would have been killed, some might have escaped, and the means of transportation to the camps would have been shattered. But American priorities were centered on beating the German army, not stopping a genocide that many American leaders remained unconvinced was even taking place.

The end of World War II in May of 1945 didn't immediately bring an end to the suffering of those in concentration camps. Tragically, many prisoners, starving and weakened by disease, died even after troops from the Soviet or American armies arrived to liberate their camps. The situation that greeted Soviet troops arriving at Auschwitz was heartbreaking. In *Hitler: Nemesis*, Ian Kershaw writes: "On January 26 [1945], an SS unit blew up the last of the crematoria in Birkenau. The next day, the SS guards retreated in heavy fighting as Soviet

A doctor assists Auschwitz concentration camp survivors leaving the Polish camp when it was liberated in January 1945.

troops liberated the 7,000 exhausted, skeleton-like prisoners they found in the Auschwitz camp-complex. They also found 368,820 men's suits, 836,244 women's coats and dresses, 5,525 pairs of women's shoes, 13,964 carpets, large quantities of children's clothes, toothbrushes, false teeth, pots and pans, and a vast amount of human hair." Many of the concentration camp prisoners healthy enough to walk when Allied forces began to close in on the camps found themselves forced into death marches through the snow by their fleeing Nazi captors. Many dropped dead as they walked. Those too weak to move on were sometimes shot by their guards. In one march from Auschwitz alone, eight hundred prisoners were murdered by their guards, sometimes for stopping briefly, sometimes for no reason whatsoever.

A SURVIVOR'S STORY

A Jewish Italian chemist and survivor of Auschwitz, Primo Levi (1919–1987) is one of the best-known and most respected contributors to the field of Holocaust literature. Levi's promising career in chemistry was cut short due to racial purity laws in Italy that prevented Italian companies from employing highly educated Jews. In 1943, he joined anti-Fascist guerrillas but was quickly captured. He was then exiled to Auschwitz because of his Jewish ancestry. He arrived at the camp with 650 other Jews from the same "shipment." Eleven months later, when the camp was liberated by the Soviet army, he was one of only twenty to have survived the experience.

After the war, Levi became a respected chemist and wrote *If This Is a Man,* an account of his time in Auschwitz. A product of Levi bearing witness to what he had seen, it was a weapon in his fight against the growing phenomenon of Holocaust denial. In 2006, Levi's *The Periodic Table,* a collection of short stories each named for a different physical element, was named the best science book ever by the Royal Institution of Great Britain.

CONTINUING MISERY

An estimated 100,000 Jewish survivors of the camps found themselves swamped amid almost seven million other uprooted and homeless European people who were classified by the Allies as displaced persons (DPs). For months, the camp survivors and other DPs wandered throughout Europe, trying to make their way home. But for the Jews—known later as *Sh'erit ha-Pletah,* a Biblical term meaning "the Surviving Remnant"—"home" was not necessarily where it used to be. Anti-Semitism and the destruction of their old communities meant that emigration to countries such as Palestine (the land that would become the modern state of Israel, which was still under the control of the British) and the United States was the only real option left.

Organized in refugee camps in Austria, Germany, and Italy, the Jewish DPs quickly organized themselves, putting together their own governing associations and cultural, educational, and social groups. As months stretched into years, they began working with the world humanitarian community to push for the British to let more Jews into Palestine and for the American government to loosen the strict immigration laws keeping Jews from coming to the United States.

CHAPTER 4

LOOKING BACK

From a modern perspective, it's difficult to wrap one's head around the fact that the horrors of the Holocaust happened. In fact, some people, known as Holocaust deniers, have argued that it could not have possibly happened based on the sheer extent of this horror. But the evidence is stacked against them. Writers and genocide victims including Elie Wiesel, Primo Levi, and Anne Frank documented their experiences during the

Anne Frank's diaries highlighted the real-life terrors faced by so many Jews during the Second World War.

Holocaust. Records from the census and the Nazis' own papers document the millions of people who vanished. Then there are the countless pieces of concrete proof, such as mass graves, the sprawling Auschwitz concentration camp compound, which is now a museum, and thousands of pairs of spectacles taken from prisoners before they were led to the gas chambers that took their lives.

HITLER'S LAWYER

A leading Nazi Party member, Hans Frank (1900–1946) rose from his position as Hitler's legal advisor to a ministerial role in the wartime German government. Frank served as governor-general for the occupied Polish territories. He was instrumental in forcing Polish Jews into the ghettos, from which they would later be shipped to the country's death camps. Hitler promised Frank, on the eve of the invasion of Russia, that Jews would be eliminated from his Polish territory.

After the war, at the Nuremburg Trials, Frank was found guilty of war crimes. Among his fellow prisoners, he was unique in accepting at least some share of guilt for what happened under his command: "My conscience does not allow me simply to throw the responsibility simply on minor people...A thousand years will pass and still Germany's guilt will not have been erased" (according to public Nuremburg Trial documents). Frank was executed in 1946.

First and foremost, the evidence collected at the post-war international tribunal held in Nuremberg represents a record—mostly written by Nazis themselves—of the massive industrial effort that was required to mount a killing campaign of the scale and intensity of the Holocaust. By holding the Nuremberg Trials, the Allied powers didn't merely bring Nazi war criminals such as Polish governor Hans Frank to account. They also ensured that the memories of the millions of people killed in the genocide would live on. The world's verdict of guilty at Nuremburg and the punishments handed down would also serve as a warning to future generations about the patterns and consequences of the Holocaust.

THE HOLOCAUST FOREVER REMEMBERED

Around the world, Holocaust museums have been built to preserve the stories of victims and survivors and to pay testament to the courage of those who challenged the Nazi regime. Some of the most significant include the Yad Vashem Memorial in Israel, the United States Holocaust Memorial Museum in Washington, D.C., and the Simon Wiesenthal Center in Los Angeles, California. All are dedicated, at least in part, to the philosophy of "Never Again"—never again should genocide stain the ground with the blood of the innocent, whatever their religion, race, or nation might be. All these museums put stories to names, helping to transform the anonymous "six million" into real people who lived, breathed, laughed, cried, worked, played, and died. The U.S. Holocaust Memorial Museum has launched

A view from inside the Community Valley Memorial for the Holocaust in the Yad Vashem Memorial in Israel

a Web project known as BENAS (Behind Every Name a Story) that allows survivors to tell their stories in essays that are then posted online. In addition, around the world, Jewish families and others observe Yom HaShoah, or Holocaust Remembrance Day. Inaugurated in 1959, Yom HaShoah is a national day of memorial in Israel.

Because of the detailed records kept by the Nazi regime and the dedication that Holocaust survivors have shown toward

A WRITER'S STORY

A French-Romanian Jewish Holocaust survivor, Elie Wiesel (b. 1928) was awarded the Nobel Peace Prize in 1986 for his work as a writer, opponent of racism, and advocate of peace. His best-known work is *Night*, the extremely influential Holocaust memoir originally published in 1958. The book is a collection of scenes from Wiesel's personal experience, such as when he was separated from his mother and sisters at Auschwitz: "For a part of a second, I glimpsed my mother and my sisters moving away to the right. Tzipora held Mother's hand. I saw them disappear into the distance; my mother was stroking my sister's fair hair ... and I did not know that in that place, at that moment, I was parting from my mother and Tzipora forever."

the mission of remembering the genocide, the Holocaust has become known throughout the world. It provides a stark warning about how ordinary people can make poor decisions and put extraordinarily bad politicians into positions of power. It also teaches of the dangerous power of language and imagery—how racist speech and images aren't merely emotionally hurtful but can also ultimately be physically destructive—as it sets the stage for far more violent crimes.

ALWAYS ON GUARD

Unfortunately, the need to remain vigilant against future geno-cides is unlikely to diminish. As long as one political group can obtain power by marginalizing and dehumanizing another, the conditions for genocide can be created. Despite the lessons learned by the world after World War II and the Holocaust, mass killings have taken place in Cambodia from 1975 to 1979 (about 1.7 million killed), Rwanda in 1994 (up to one million killed), and Darfur (an estimated 200,000 to 450,000 people dead of disease or killed in violence). So the fight continues even today, with Holocaust survivors and their descendants

The United States Holocaust Memorial Museum in Washington, D.C., highlights genocides and people struggling in other countries, too, such as this display about the Rohingya Muslims in Burma.

active in the effort to call attention to and halt genocidal killing wherever it may take place.

The United States Holocaust Memorial Museum's Committee on Conscience has played an active role in alerting the public to possible genocides or genocides in progress, such as in Darfur in recent years. Formed as a living memorial to the Holocaust, the group's mandate is to "alert the national conscience, influence policy makers, and stimulate worldwide action to confront and work to halt acts of genocide or related crimes against humanity." Groups like the Committee on Conscience are active around the world, and the memory of the Holocaust fuels their fight.

1889 Adolf Hitler is born.

1914 Germany enters World War I.

1918 Germany capitulates to the Allies, ending World War I.

1923 The Nazi Party's Beer Hall Putsch, an attempt to seize power in Germany, fails; Hitler receives a light jail sentence.

1925 *Mein Kampf*, Hitler's autobiography, is published.

1933 The Nazi Party comes to power in Germany. Laws are passed to ban Jews from practicing medicine or law, attending universities, belonging to the Journalists' Association, joining the Civil Service, or owning a farm. Dachau, one of the first concentration camps, is opened.

1935 Hitler introduces the Nuremberg Laws.

1938 During Kristallnacht, thousands of Jewish businesses and places of worship are destroyed.

1939 Germany occupies Poland, putting about two million more Jews under Nazi control.

1940 The Warsaw ghetto is established; many die from disease and starvation there.

1941 During the Iasi pogrom in Romania, police and Romanian citizens kill as many as fourteen thousand Jews. More than thirty-three thousand Jews are killed by Germans and police in the Babi Yar massacre outside of Kiev, Ukraine. The first fatal gassings of concentration camp prisoners take place in Auschwitz.

1942 The Wannsee Conference in Berlin is convened, and the decision is made to concentrate all of Europe's Jews into labor camps, with the intention of killing some or all of them. Six major concentration camps are fully operational in Poland. The Warsaw Ghetto is partially emptied, and three hundred thousand people are sent to the Treblinka extermination camp.

1943 Ghetto uprisings (including the Warsaw Ghetto Uprising) try and fail to prevent mass deportations through armed resistance.

1944 Jewish Sonderkommandos at Auschwitz stage an uprising; 250 Jews escape, but all are eventually recaptured and killed. Germany occupies Hungary, putting another eight hundred thousand Jews under Nazi control; more than half are shipped to Auschwitz, where most die. Oskar Schindler writes his famous, life-saving list.

1945 Death marches reach a peak. All remaining concentration camps are liberated by Allied forces. The war ends with Germany's total defeat by the Allies. Nuremberg Trials of German war criminals begin. Hitler commits suicide in Berlin, Germany.

1948 The Jewish state of Israel is founded.

1983 Thomas Keneally's book *Schindler's List* is published.

1993 The U.S. Holocaust Memorial Museum is dedicated and opened in Washington, D.C.

2004 The U.S. Holocaust Memorial Museum and the American Jewish World Service initiate the Save Darfur Coalition, a group of 150 faith-based advocacy and humanitarian aid groups dedicated to halting the genocide in Darfur, Sudan.

2007 The Jewish Council for Public Affairs places the Darfur genocide crisis at the top of its political agenda, officially making the issue a top priority for the Jewish community.

Allies In World War II, the major Allied powers included Britain, France, the Soviet Union, and the United States. They fought the Axis powers (Germany, Italy, and Japan).

concentration camp Generally some combination of prison, slave labor camp, extermination camp, and crematory (where bodies were burned).

Einsatzgruppen Mobile groups of gunmen under the command of the SS who killed many Jews in the East (Russia, the Baltic States, Ukraine).

Final Solution Hitler's plan for what he called the "Jewish problem," which referred to the complete extermination of all of Europe's Jews.

genocide The deliberate destruction of an ethnic, religious, and/or national group.

Gestapo Hitler's feared secret police, a contraction of the German words for "secret state police."

Hebrew The ancient language of the Jewish people of Israel.

Kristallnacht (Night of Broken Glass) A night of voilence against Jews and their property on November 10, 1938.

Mein Kampf In English, "My Struggle." Hitler's autobiography, which warned of many of his future plans for Germany, including military expansion, and his hatred of Jews.

Nuremberg Laws A series of laws introduced by Hitler in 1935 that deprived Jews of their citizenship and civil rights, leaving them vulnerable to violence and imprisonment in concentration camps.

Nuremberg Trials Trials held from 1945 to 1949 in Nuremberg, Germany. The United States, the Soviet Union, and Great Britain were key in creating and overseeing the trials, in which roughly two hundred Germans were tried for war crimes.

pogrom A riot directed against members of a specific group, typically an ethnic or religious minority.

propaganda Information designed to help one political party gain and retain power.

Shoah A Hebrew word that literally means "calamity." Among many Jews, it is the preferred way to refer to what is commonly called the Holocaust.

Sonderkommandos Jewish work units forced to assist in the killings at the concentration camps.

Soviet Union A collection of states headed by what is now Russia, but including the Ukraine, the Baltic republics, and numerous central Asian states. The Soviet Union was unified by the Communist Party, which maintained a lock on its government until its disintegration in 1991.

SS Two letters that stand for "Schutzstaffel," which is German for "protective squadron." The SS was one of Nazi Germany's most feared military organizations. SS men staffed the concentration camps, serving as guards and administrators.

Yad Vashem Israel's official museum dedicated to preserving the memory of those who perished in (or survived) the Holocaust.

Canadian Jewish Congress Charities Committee (CJCCC)
1590 Docteur Penfield Avenue
Montreal, QB H3G 1C5
Canada
(514) 931-7531, ext. 2
Website: http://www.cjccc.ca
The Canadian Jewish Congress Charities Committee
(CJCCC) National Archives is a collection of all aspects of
Jewish life in Canada.

Canadian Jewish Holocaust Survivors & Descendents
4600 Bathurst Street, 4th Floor
Toronto, ON M6A 3V2
Canada
In cooperation with the Centre for Israel and Jewish Affairs
(CIJA), the Canadian Jewish Holocaust Survivors & Descen-
dents organization serves as a voice for Holocaust survivors
to ensure they are always remembered.

Holocaust Education Foundation
64 Old Orchard Road
Professional Building, Suite 520
Skokie, IL 60077
(847) 676-3700
Website: http://www.holocaustef.org
The Holocaust Educational Foundation is a private, non-profit

organization established in 1980 by survivors, their children, and their friends to preserve and promote awareness of the reality of the Holocaust.

Holocaust Teacher Resource Center
P.O. Box 6153
Newport News, VA 23606-6153
Website: http://www.holocaust-trc.org
The Holocaust Teacher Resource Center strives to combat prejudice and bigotry by transforming the horrors of the Holocaust into positive lessons to help make this a better and safer world for everybody.

The Jewish Foundation for the Righteous
305 Seventh Avenue, 19th Floor
New York, NY 10001-6008
(212) 727-9955
Website: http://www.jfr.org
This foundation provides financial assistance to aged and needy non-Jews who risked their lives to save Jews during the Holocaust. It also educates teachers and students about the Holocaust.

Survivors of the Shoah Visual History Foundation
P.O. Box 3168
Los Angeles, CA 90078-3168
(818) 777-7802
Website: http://www.vhf.org
This institute has an archive of nearly fifty-two thousand vid-

eotaped testimonies from Holocaust survivors and other witnesses. It works with a global network of partners to provide an array of valuable educational services.

United States Holocaust Memorial Museum
100 Raoul Wallenberg Place SW
Washington, DC 20024-2126
(202) 488-0400
Website: http://www.ushmm.org
The museum's Center for Advanced Holocaust Studies works to ensure the continued growth and vitality of the field of Holocaust studies and prevent genocide in the future through the Academy for Genocide Prevention, which trains foreign policy professionals.

Yad Vashem
POB 3477
Jerusalem
Israel 9103401
Website: http://www.yadvashem.org
This Israeli organization is dedicated to the Holocaust.

WEBSITES

Because of the changing nature of Internet links, Rosen Publishing has developed an online list of websites related to the subject of this book. This site is updated regularly. Please use this link to access the list:
http://www.rosenlinks.com/BWGE/holo

Brezina, Corona. *Nazi Architects of the Holocaust* (A Documentary History of the Holocaust). New York, NY: Rosen Publishers, 2014.

Des Chenes, Elizabeth, ed. *Genocide* (Contemporary Issues Companion). Farmington Hills, MI: Greenhaven, 2007.

Frank, Anne. *The Diary of a Young Girl.* New York, NY: Spark Publishing, 2014.

Gratz, Alan. *Prisoner B-3087.* New York, NY: Scholastic Press, 2013.

Keneally, Thomas. *Schindler's List.* New York, NY: Touchstone, 2013.

Levi, Primo, and Raymond Rosenthal. *The Periodic Table.* Camberwell, Victoria, Australia: Penguin, 2012.

Levi, Primo. *Surviving Auschwitz.* New York, NY: Barnes & Noble, 2007.

Opdyke, Irene. *In My Hands: Memories of a Holocaust Rescuer.* New York, NY: Laurel Leaf, 2008.

Rappaport, Doreen. *Beyond Courage: The Untold Story of Jewish Resistance During the Holocaust.* Somerville, MA: Candlewick Press, 2014.

Roy, Jennifer. *Yellow Star.* Allentown, PA: Two Lions, 2014.

Spiegelman, Art. *The Complete Maus: A Survivior's Tale.* 25th anniversary ed. New York, NY: Pantheon Books, 2011.

Wiesel, Elie. *Dawn.* New York, NY: Hill & Wang, 2013.

Wiesel, Elie. *Day.* New York, NY: Hill & Wang, 2006.

Wiesel, Elie. *Night.* New York, NY: Hill & Wang, 2006.

Bauer, Yehuda. *Rethinking the Holocaust.* New Haven, CT: Yale University Press, 2001.

Berenbaum, Michael. *The World Must Know.* Washington, DC: United States Holocaust Museum, 2006.

Crowe, David M. *Oskar Schindler: The Untold Account of His Life, Wartime Activities, and the True Story Behind the List.* Philadelphia, PA: Westview Press, 2004.

Dwork, Deborah, and Robert Jan van Pelt. *Holocaust: A History.* New York, NY: W.W. Norton and Co., 2002.

Goldhagen, Daniel Jonah. *Hitler's Willing Executioners: Ordinary Germans and the Holocaust.* New York, NY: Alfred A. Knopf, 1996.

Greene, Joshua M., and Shiva Kumar. *Witness: Voices from the Holocaust.* New York, NY: The Free Press, 2000.

Iranek-Osmecki, Kazimierz. *He Who Saves One Life: The Complete, Documented Story of the Poles Who Struggled to Save Jews During World War Two.* New York, NY: Crown, 1971.

Kershaw, Ian. *Hitler: 1889–1936 Hubris.* New York, NY: W.W. Norton and Co., 1999.

Kershaw, Ian. Hitler: 1936–1945 Nemesis. New York, NY: W.W. Norton and Co., 2000.

Lowery, Zoe, and Jeremy Roberts. *Oskar Schindler* (The Holocaust). New York, NY Rosen Publishing, 2015.

Museum of Tolerance. "Timeline of the Holocaust." 2014

(http://www.museumoftolerance.com/site/c.tmL6KfN-VLtH/b.5879251/k.72C8/Timeline_of_the_Holocaust.htm).

Pringle, Heather. *The Master Plan: Himmler's Scholars and the Holocaust.* New York, NY: Hyperion, 2006.

Segev, Tom. *The Seventh Million: The Israelis and the Holocaust.* New York, NY: Henry Holt and Co., 1991.

World Atlas. "Populations of World's 100 Largest Cities." 2015 (http://www.worldatlas.com/citypops.htm).

INDEX

ABOUT THE AUTHORS

Zoe Lowery is an avid student of history, constantly reading and studying about the past and other thought-provoking topics. She has written and edited a number of books on the topic for Rosen Publishing. Lowery lives in Colorado.

James Norton is a writer based in Minneapolis, Minnesota. He holds a degree in history from the University of Wisconsin-Madison and has worked as an international news editor, political journalist, and food writer. He is the founder and editor of *Flak Magazine* (www.flakmag.com).

PHOTO CREDITS

Cover (photo) Sovfoto/Universal Images Group/Getty Images; cover (cracked texture) Marbury/Shutterstock.com; p. 5 Sylvain Sonnet/Photolibrary/Getty Images; pp. 7, 20, 36 Hulton Archive/Getty Images; p. 11 Heinrich Hoffmann/Hulton Archive/Getty Images; p. 13 Keystone-France/Gamma-Keystone/Getty Images; pp. 14–15 FPG/Archive Photos/Getty Images; pp. 18, 45 ullstein bild/Getty Images; pp. 22, 31, 34, 38–39 Universal History Archive/UIG/Getty Images; p. 27 Fred Ramage/Hulton Archive/Getty Images; p. 42 Heritage Images/Hulton Archive/Getty Images; p. 48 Karin Wabro/Shutterstock.com; p. 50 © AP Images; back cover, pp. 13, 18, 19, 24, 26, 32, 38, 39, 40, 43, 46, 49 (skulls) rangizzz/Shutterstock.com; pp. 7, 17, 29, 45 (top) pimchawee/Shutterstock.com; additional background textures Reinhold Leitner/Shutterstock.com, © iStockphoto.com/ShutterWorx.
Designer: Brian Garvey; Photo Researcher: Heather Moore Niver